Confronting Life:

The 7 Questions on the Minds of
Believers and Non-Believers

John Adjei

DEDICATION

To believers and sceptics, hoping they will read!

CONTENTS

Introduction 1

Why I wrote this Book 3

Question 1: Why are human beings never satisfied with all the material opportunities life has to offer? 6

Question 2: Does the Bible have any truth?..25

Question 3: Is Christ's resurrection literally true? 35

Question 4: Is Christianity a Kingdom or a religion? 51

Question 5: Saved, what next? 60

Question 6: What ought to be the priority in life? 67

Question 7: What is the best view of success? 75

Answers to Activities Questions 85

About the Author 100

Introduction

As human beings, at some point or another, we all experience emptiness, loneliness, dissatisfaction, and a longing for something to fill the void we feel within us. Many look to fill this abyss with material things, like sex, drugs, money, power, fame, work, or stuff, which admittedly can help us escape or mask the pain temporarily. Unfortunately, it is never enough, and for most, the outcome is more dissatisfaction and even an eventual decline into self-destruction, if the situation is not remedied.

You can see this everywhere you look, from Wall Street to Hollywood, to your friends, family and co-workers, and maybe even yourself, if you are honest.

So why is this problem so universal, and how

do we free ourselves from its bonds? The answer is quite simple, and it all comes down to just two things: connecting with the source of life and living your purpose.

I know this is true because I have found purpose in my own life, and now life is more exciting, meaningful, and fulfilling than ever before.

Mind you, this didn't happen overnight, and throughout my life I have faced the same struggles of discontent and unfulfillment you have. But after over 30 years of studying and living the lessons of the Bible, I have formulated a set of ideas that can help anyone overcome a sense of meaningless and despair and start to live purposely with a sense of accomplishment, joy and peace.

The best news is, this is not a quick fix and it is not difficult to do. It is permanent and everlasting, and it is available to everyone, right now, just by reading this guide to confronting life.

Why I wrote this book

Having served as an educator in the UK university sector for over 10 years, I have become increasingly aware of the importance, the usefulness, and the benefits of asking questions. Students cannot be promoted to the next stage of their studies without being subjected to some form of questioning or questions. On the other hand, students gain enormously by asking questions. Interrogating further with questions is one of the best ways we learn. Some of the benefits of asking the right questions are as follows:

- We get more relevant information.

- We get more intelligent.

- We get a better understanding and become wiser.

- We increase our chances to be more successful and happier.

Similarly, through questioning, all of us as students of life stand a better chance to gain new knowledge, clarity and understanding on which we can act and take the right and informed actions.

I am very much aware that many people have many questions in this fallen world of uncertainties, rife with meaninglessness, driving many to desperation and wretchedness.

I hope some of the answers to some of these seven questions will be useful and help ameliorate some of the anxiety-provoking thoughts and answer some of the questions people have in life, and about the Christian faith in particular.

I do acknowledge that the answers to the seven questions in this book are not exhaustive, but I hope they are good enough to inspire action to help you become your best.

Each question is followed by three activities to guide you to deeply reflect and engage with the ideas in this book so as to get the most from it. Suggested guidelines to these activities are also provided after question 7.

So if you are ready, let us begin.

Question 1: Why are human beings never satisfied with all the material opportunities life has to offer?

Suggested Answer to Question 1

The short answer is that material things do not offer sustainable satisfaction. This is proven in economics by the *Richard Easterlin paradox*.

This world is not devised to make us happy but to challenge us to awaken to our authentic selves where true fulfilment lies. We discover possibilities and find meaning when we take up our *cross*, embrace responsibility and confront challenges in life.

There is a personal story to this question. This question came up in one of our family's weekly meetings where we catch up with each other, discuss life issues based on the Bible, and answer questions that come up.

A young girl in her late teens had unfortunately committed suicide, and this had gone viral. We can all identify with someone we know or close to us who has taken their own life and the feeling of grief that follows such unfortunate circumstances. My children, who are in their early teens, were feeling this grief for her and her family and were also feeling some form of confusion, having many unanswered questions on their minds. This is the conversation we had:

Daughter: Dad, have you heard of the girl who ended her life this week?

Dad: Yes, but I have no recollection of the details. This is so sad, and I can only pray for the family, as they may be having a difficult time right now.

Daughter: The family and the world did not even have the opportunity to see what she had to offer.

Dad: Tell me, what happened to her?

Daughter: It appears she thought she was in genuine love with an adult only to realise that she had been used and sexually abused by this unscrupulous, run-away adult, and the shame was too much for her.

Dad: This is so sad and unfortunate.

Daughter: Her parents were well-to-do and provided her with all the material things she needed. She had her room, the latest laptop, a smartphone, other posh gadgets, and all she asked the parents for. What, then, drove her to this wicked man that started her unfortunate journey of no return?

Dad: What do you think, Daughter? [This allowed me more time as I had no immediate answer.] Oh God, please help me [I murmured]. [The whole family remained silent for a moment.]

Daughter: I don't know.

Dad: There is a story in the Bible about a Samaritan woman's encounter with Jesus which may help to answer your question.

Daughter: Are you sure?

Dad: Sure! Can we quickly read the story in John 4:1–42 and see similar patterns to this girl's story?

[The family spent a few minutes checking the story in curiosity.]

Daughter: Jesus is asking for water, and this woman is reluctant to give some to him. But what has this story got to do with the question about a girl who had sought love only to realise it was not genuine?

Dad: If we dig deep to uncover the timeless truth in this story in the scriptures, we will notice the patterns played out exactly as seen in the girl's story.

Daughter: How?

Dad: Let me explain. First, this story is not about literal water. The thirst and search for water are being used as an illustration of an essential and fundamental truth about all of us (the human race), and we ignore it at our peril.

Dad: This Samaritan woman's continual search and regular visit to the well for water shows the *human condition* after the fall out of mankind with the Creator. There is a *void*, *vacuum*, *emptiness*, or loneliness described as a '*thirst*' in the human soul/spirit (deep within us), and this spiritual void or thirst can only be fully and eternally satisfied by Christ (God) through the 'supernatural water' he offers to all humanity. Below is Jesus' response to the woman's reluctance to give some of her natural water to him:

Jesus answered and said to her, 'Whoever drinks of this water will thirst again, but whoever drinks of the water that I shall give him will never thirst. But the water that I shall give him will become in him a fountain of water springing up into everlasting life' (John 4:13–14 NKJV).

Jesus replied, 'Anyone who drinks this water will soon become thirsty again. But those who drink the water I give will never be thirsty again. It becomes a fresh, bubbling spring within them, giving them eternal life' (John 4:13–14 NLT).

Daughter: Then everybody needs this water!

Dad: That's right! In fact, in the absence of Christ (God), the default for human beings is to satisfy this feeling of a void inside of us on our own terms by trying some pseudo-escapes or pseudo-substitutes such as money, sex, drugs, fame, and power. These are essential things God gave mankind as tools to serve good purposes. The problem is when they are used out of the proper context and not for the intended purpose, and are an obsession to quench our thirst and to replace the sacred position in our heart only meant for God. What follows such a choice is that we get addicted, entangled and controlled, and problems, pain, self-inflicted and unnecessary suffering, and the eventual demolishing of ourselves are the natural, inevitable consequences.

Daughter: So what was the pseudo-substitute evident in either story?

Dad: Like many of us, the Samaritan woman thought the answer to quenching her thirst was to be found in men (sex). She had tried it in five previous marriages to no avail, and she was on her sixth sexual relationship, all in pursuit of true *agape love* that only God can give because he is Love (1 John 4:8, 4:16). So do you now notice the similarities of this woman in the Bible and the story of the poor girl?

Daughter: Yeah! From the available information, it seems like the innocently naïve girl felt lonely or empty on the inside, and the attempt to satisfy this void led her to the selfish man who promised her love, which turned out to be an infatuation and lust in disguise. Unfortunately, she did not appear to have had a personal relationship with Jesus, who fills our hearts with joy and assurance of a fulfilled life.

Dad: Brilliant! So what other lessons have you learned?

Daughter: Without Christ, no human being (parent, teacher, spouse, friend, expert, celebrity, royal, boyfriend/girlfriend) or any material thing can make me fully satisfied in life.

Dad: True! The ultimate lesson of this story is that we all need Jesus to forgive and lift off the burden of sin, reconcile us to our source (God, our Father), and provide us irreplaceable 'supernatural water' to quench our otherwise insatiable thirst and give us satisfaction, fulfilment, certainty, and everlasting life starting right here, right now.

Jesus is not just a unique teacher, prophet, historical or religious figure, but a transcendent Living Power with whom everyone needs a personal encounter like this Samaritan woman. Each adult needs their own personal, firsthand experience of his presence, which is full of inner peace and joy. He is *the way* that leads us to *the truth* that gives us *a fulfilled life*.

There is no substitute for Christ and the peace he offers our soul. Kanye West, in his confession in his YouTube videos,[1] said he tried fame, sex, and money, and all failed him. It was only after accepting Jesus into his heart that he found joy in his soul. Today, many are trying drugs to quench their 'thirst', not knowing there is *no high* like the *Most High*. We all need Him because distance from Him is hell, a hellish experience we initiate right now, right here on earth.

In this story is Jesus' gracious, all-inclusive invitation to the whole human race (you, me and others), to drink of this transcendent water in Him that can fully quench our thirst. He wants us to turn away from pseudo-substitutes like material things or another human who is limited, fallible, and will die one day. Instead, he wants us to look to him, a *perfect human*, a person who is *fully human* and *fully God*. He came from Heaven to our material world to experience the suffering we go through so he could identify with us and provide our number

---

[1] 'Kanye West's Born-Again Testimony', available on YouTube at: https://www.youtube.com/watch?v=zMqqTzwErb8&t=86s.

one need for our soul and the courage and capacity to transcend suffering. By saying yes to his offer as this Samaritan woman did, we kickstart a living, personal, and intimate relationship that will fully satisfy us, and this satisfaction will last forever.

Daughter: Dad, do we have any recent real-life, evidence-based research to support the claim Jesus made to this woman in this story?

Dad: Oh yeah! The benefits of following Jesus Christ are abundantly self-evident. In October 2016, professor Tyler J. VanderWeele of Harvard School of Public Health and journalist John Siniff published the surprising physical and mental health benefits of regular church attendance in *USA Today*. From over 20 years of study, they discovered that *followers of Christ are more optimistic*, have lower rates of depression, have less tendency to commit suicide or divorce, are more purpose-driven, and exercise more self-control. All this culminates in reducing Christians' mortality rates by about 20–30 per cent over a 15-year period, and they termed these benefits *a miracle drug*.[2]

The enormous positive externality and ripple effects from such individual actions to families and society as a whole should call for support for following Christ rather than secularisation, whose rise will be a recipe for public-health and meaning crises. It seems like this has already started to manifest right in front of our eyes with the unfortunately rampant acceleration of mental health problems and suicide.

There is also a moving story by two ex-Muslim girls who found this water in Jesus to satisfy their thirst when they had a personal encounter with him. They experienced Jesus' peace, presence, and power that helped alleviate the unbearable suffering they had to endure just because of their newly found faith in Christ. Their story, which attracted the intervention of the Pope and Christian civil rights activists

---

[2] Professor Tyler J. VanderWeele of Harvard School of Public Health and John Siniff, '*Religion May Be a Miracle Drug*', October 2016, Available at: https://eu.usatoday.com/story/opinion/2016/10/28/religion-church-attendance-mortality-column/92676964/.

around the world, is in their book *Captive in Iran*.[3]

Mark Koch, a successful Hollywood movie producer, is someone with another dramatic story of an encounter with Christ. In his response to the peace, joy and meaning found in Christ, he has dedicated *The First Hour*[4] of every day to learning more about Jesus, and he is urging Americans to do the same.

Daughter: Dad, what do you have to say to my friends who say they do not need any God(s), they just want to be free and true to themselves?

Dad: Great question! This may be on the minds of many people out there.

First, there is a *Freedom Myth*. Let me explain. Even though we have our willpower, we are not totally in charge of our lives. There are

---

[3] Maryam Rostampour and Marziyeh Amirizadeh (2013), *Captive in Iran: Remarkable True Story of Hope and Triumph Amid the Horror of Tehran's Brutal Evin Prison*, Tyndale House Publishers.
[4] Mark Koch's story, available at: https://thefirsthour.com/.

forces in and around us that transcend us, and control us. This explains why some people get into the bondage of addictions[5].

We are moved to live for something and whatever thing we decide to live for, other than Christ, enslaves us. Over time, the absence of fulfilment eventually makes us feel inadequate, guilty and shameful like it happened to this Samaritan woman before she found Jesus. Although slavery and liberty can be seen as socially constructed to some extent, we all seem to have been born slaves to our feelings, inordinate desires, our passions, our ego, and the circumstances of the human condition.

Jesus is the only good master who can fully satisfy, and even if we fail, he will forgive us and empower us to be truly free. *With him, our story line is guaranteed a happy ending.*

Dad: Regarding being true to oneself, it is in Christ that we rediscover our true, authentic

---

[5] Romans 6:16 (NLT): "Don't you realize that you become the slave of whatever you choose to obey? You can be a slave to sin, which leads to death, or you can choose to obey God, which leads to righteous living."

selves. Our original identity and who we truly are has been distorted in this fallen world. This has led to the formation of many identities creating identity crisis in our world today.

The identity found in Christ is the only *superior identity* that is *received* and not achieved. It takes the pressure off our shoulders from playing an identity for love, acceptance, self-gratification, and significance.

If your friends want an identity which is true, and not exclusive, and can serve as a basis for social and economic justice, meaning and fulfilment, it is to be found in Jesus Christ.

When we discover our identity in Christ, we find uncommon forgiveness so we can easily forgive others. In Christ, we find genuine acceptance so we can accept others. In Christ, we find unconditional love so we have the power to love people with God's kind of love.

I am well aware that the above exposition on the story in John 4 is never all there is to the story. There are many truths and principles to be abstracted to guide our lives. If approached with an open heart and the respect and reverent attitude it deserves, another layer of truth may be revealed to you and your specific situation and be applicable to your sphere of influence, whether this is in business, politics, entertainment, health, education, media, sports, religion, or whatever you are engaged in.

For example, a sociological view reveals how Jesus punched a hole in racism and racial discrimination and marginalisation. The Jews at the time did not have anything to do with the Samaritans. There was a rift between them, and they hated each other, with the Jews having an attitude towards the Samaritans. So for Jesus to strike a mutually respectful conversation, make himself vulnerable by asking for help, and engage this woman was a radical departure from the entrenched discrimination and marginalisation of other groups at the time. This embracing action was a bold statement in support of the idea that we are all created equal and bear the same image of God regardless of our race or sex. Jesus did set the records straight, affirming that *Samaritan lives matter*, Black lives matter, every life matters, and that there is only one race, the human race.

Human beings have created many classes based on tribes, ethnicity, nationality, socio-economic status, religious or political affiliation, and the rest that divide us. To God, the entire human race is his offspring and is part of just one of two groups: *believers* and *non-believers*, those who choose and trust him, and those who reject him. He does not see us around human divisions such as black and white or anything in-between, rich and poor, men and women but through the two lenses of saints and sinners.

In his *New York Times* bestselling book, Tim Keller, a brilliant Christian apologist and co-founder of *Redeem City to City*, which trains pastors for ministry in global cities, agrees that to make sense of life and to understand the world, one needs to understand Jesus by reading the Gospels (the first four books in the

New Testament: Matthew, Mark, Luke and John).[6]

The story also reveals that God knows everything about every person and all they have ever done: the good, the bad, and the ugly, but he is willing to forgive, accept and empower us if we turn to him.

Will you accept this invitation today?

_____

[6] Tim Keller (2008), *The Reason for God: Belief in an Age of Scepticism,* USA, Penguin Group.

Activities based on Question and Answer 1

1. Like this Samaritan woman, do you want to accept Jesus' free offer?

2. Why do you need Jesus?

3. What happens to life without Jesus?

Why are human beings never satisfied ...?

Question 2: Does the Bible have any truth?

Suggested Answer to Question 2

It depends on what we mean by truth. Everyone in the world is in search of the truth. Science is in pursuit of truth. So it might be worthwhile to explore the question, what is truth?

From Wikipedia, *truth is being in accord with fact or reality or being in accord with an original.*[7] Two types

---

of truth are encapsulated in this definition:

- *Objective truth* – explored by science, and
- *Phenomenological truth* – embodied, personified and demonstrated by Christ.

Based on the creation account in the Bible, the original of the human race is God, and He made us according to His image and likeness.[8] Christ, who pre-existed as the Word[9] with Him, emerges as the Son of God to show us how to act like the Original.[10] Until an individual comes to this understanding, they are unlikely to know who they really are, and in the absence of this truth, life is meaningless.

Objective or *scientific truth* studies *matter* and the objects in the universe and helps us understand what the world is made up of. *Phenomenological truth*, on the other hand, studies *what matters*:

---

[8] Genesis 1:26 (NKJV): "Then God said, 'Let Us make man in Our image, according to Our likeness'".

[9] John 1:1 (NKJV): 'In the beginning was the Word, and the Word was with God, and the Word was God'.

[10] Colossians 1:15—18 (NKJV): 'He **[Jesus]** is the image of the invisible God, the firstborn **[Model]** over all creation'. Emphasis added.

what it means to be human, how we experience the human consciousness, how to live, and the living experience. It is just like a science student who excels at an anatomy exam because they know the human body. However, this knowledge does not inform the purpose of the human being. What does this is the *phenomenological truth*, which is embedded in the stories in the Bible.

The entire Bible narrative is one coherent story about one person, Jesus Christ, who emphasised his *deity* and claimed what no human being or any religious leader on earth has ever dared to say: '*I am the Truth*'.[11] Christ is the *phenomenological truth* – the Truth about how to live this life, which can be seen in human beings as the best reflection of Christ an individual can manage to manifest in reality. In different words, the *Truth is the degree to which a person allows the Spirit of Christ to manifest through them*.

When we follow Christ, the Truth, his Spirit

---

[11] John 14:6 (NKJV): 'I am the way, the truth, and the life'.

leads us to all Truths.[12] This proves why the pursuit of the Truth in Christ led the early-century Christian leaders to come up with the idea of higher education and to start research institutions which have become the top, most-prestigious global universities we have today. They founded Harvard, Yale, Princeton, and others (in the USA), and Oxford, Cambridge, and Saint Andrews (in the UK)[13] initially as institutes for Christian studies to discover more Truths. Secular humanities were added along later. For example, one of the faculties or schools in the University of Cambridge is *Christ's College* which has produced influential thinkers like Charles Darwin, was founded as *God's House* in 1437 by a vicar called William Byngham[14].

In her Christian apologetic masterclass book

---

[12] John 16:13 (NKJV): 'When He, the Spirit of truth, has come, He will guide you into all truth'.

[13] Answers in Genesis, and *Forbes* – Available at: https://answersingenesis.org/christianity/harvard-yale-princeton-oxford-once-christian/, https://www.forbes.com/sites/cartercoudriet/2016/07/19/top-25-christian-colleges-the-essential-questions-on-religion-and-education/.

[14] Available at: https://en.wikipedia.org/wiki/Christ%27s_College,_Cambridge

answering the question *Aren't We Better off without Religion?*, Rebecca Mclaughlin, a British female with a PhD from Cambridge, confirms that Christians invented university and science, so it is strange and paradoxical that science is seen today as antithetical to Christianity.[15] We owe the Scientific Revolution to Christ and his followers, and anyone who has benefitted from higher education in any way, shape or form should forever be grateful to Christ and Christians. The key role played by the Christian Reformers (the Protestants) in facilitating the Industrial Revolution is also well known.

So the idea that science has disproved the Bible is not only ridiculously untrue but impossible. This is because each one presents different aspects of Truth. Science advances the cause of *objective truth*, while the Bible has *phenomenological truth*.

The Bible has also got *Spiritual truth* – not yet visible or perceptible by our *five senses* of seeing by the eye or brain, smelling by the nose,

---

[15] Rebecca McLaughlin (2019), *Confronting Christianity: 12 Hard Questions for the World's Largest Religions*, Wheaton, Crossway Books.

29

tasting by the tongue, touching by the hands, and feeling by the body. Spiritual truth is perceivable by the *6th sense*, that is, *faith by the heart*. For example, I usually notice enormous potential in some of the students I teach on Newcastle University preparatory courses. At the beginning, it is difficult for most of the students to believe when they are told about their potential because they cannot see or perceive by the five senses what they are capable of accomplishing. It takes believing first, backed by corresponding action before the physical evidence is seen. What gives me most fulfilment in my teaching career is when I see the transformation in the students who believe in their potential, and work hard to manifest it.

This *spiritual truth* or principle is self-evidently true. Everything visible comes from the invisible realm. Every business in existence today started as an invisible idea or spiritual truth in the mind of someone.

The problem most of us have is our inability to exercise our 6th, *spiritual sense*, the faith to perceive our potential. Without the faith to believe in our potential and the spiritual truth about ourselves, there is no motivation to work hard and to even try. Failure and mediocre follow as the natural self-fulfilling outcome of our lack of faith.

The Bible reveals *Spiritual truth*, principles and realities about life which cannot be realised by our body or mind, but by faith accessible only to the spirit part of our tripartite being[16].

Great Christian scientists like Isaac Newton and Galileo Galilei, as well as the influential psychologists and philosophers such as Carl Jung, have long maintained that *if there is any conflict between science and the Bible, it is a mere consequence of our immature state of both domains of thinking* and that a deeper understanding will reveal no contradictions, but complementarity. '*Galileo argued that proper interpretation of Scripture*

---

[16] 1 Thessalonians 5:23 (NKJV): "… may your whole spirit, soul, and body be preserved blameless at the coming of our Lord Jesus Christ."

would agree with observed facts.'[17]

Jordan B. Peterson, a professor of psychology at the University of Toronto, who is considered the most influential thinker in the world today,[18] has made an outstandingly brilliant attempt to reconcile science and the Bible in his *Biblical Series I: Introduction to the Idea of God*[19] on YouTube, which draws on the works of influential thinkers such as Dostoevsky and Nietzsche.

So the Bible is a unique book with stories and parables that convey important truths about the living experience that are easily memorable and relatable. *Embedded in the Bible is phenomenological and spiritual truths to govern and transform our lives.* It is Divinely inspired[20] and written to our heart, not just our head. The inspired text is closed and only opens its layers

---

[17] Sunday Adelaja (2007), *Church Shift Guide*, Southlake, Resolute Books: Page 76.
[18] Quora.com, available at: https://www.quora.com/Is-Jordan-Peterson-the-most-influential-thinker-in-the-western-world-today.
[19] Jordan Peterson, available at: https://www.youtube.com/watch?v=f-wWBGo6a2w&t=8014s.
[20] 2 Timothy 3:16 (NKJV): 'All Scripture *is* given by inspiration of God, and *is* profitable for doctrine, for reproof, for correction, for instruction in righteousness'.

of truth to those who approach it with a heart of sincerity and humility.

Anyone who wants to live their best and close to the *Original* should follow *Christ*, who is not only the Son of God but also the *archetype* of the ideal human being. He is the main *hero* in the stories in the Bible. We can abstract *his nature*, *principles*, and *priorities*, and follow his steps to emulate him to the degree possible. This enables us to undergo a complete transformation to become our true, authentic and best selves.

Activities based on Question and Answer 2

1. What is the danger for a person who does not discover the *phenomenological truth* in Christ in the Bible?

2. How were our ancestors able to survive without much knowledge of *scientific* or *objective truth*?

3. List three lessons you have learned and show how you are going to apply them to your life.

Question 3: Is Christ's resurrection literally true?

Suggested Answer to Question 3

Everything about Christ is supernatural – the virgin birth, the numerous, mind-blowing miracles, the circumstances surrounding his death, resurrection and ascension. If there is God Almighty who is not limited by time, space or matter, why should we have a problem with his Son, who also transcends our natural limitations?

In our limited natural realm, which is not all there is to reality, these verifiable historical records about Jesus do not lend themselves to logical reasoning alone. So the best approach is to carefully examine the evidence on both sides of the argument and decide to either believe or reject.

To fully comprehend the resurrection, it might be worthwhile to briefly explore why Jesus had to die in the first place. Many scriptures, particularly those in the Gospel of John, show the pre-existence of Jesus to the effect that the world was made through him. Even though God never intended for the human beings He had created to share His agape love in a loving relationship to experience evil and die, He knew before creation through His omniscience that, given the free will to choose, the first humankind (Adam), who was carrying the entire human race, would sin (disobedience to God's Word), rebel, and inevitably bring evil and death (which starts from separation from God) to this earth. And since the rebellion[21], human beings have been living in a fallen state and nature that naturally gravitate towards evil. We all sin, no one is good relative to God's

---

[21] This account is in Genesis chapters 1 to 3

perfect standards[22], and justice demands that sin is punishable by death[23]. So out of His compassion, mercy and love for the human race, God pre-planned the substitutionary death of Jesus to justly atone for our sins so we can be forgiven and reunited with Him[24]. Jesus' death resolves the issue of our sins which separate us from God. Now, it is no longer good or bad people who are accepted by God but only forgiven people or those who do not reject the forgiveness and salvation Jesus offers for all humanity.

There will be no Christianity without the death and the resurrection of Christ. The whole edifice of Christianity is built on the pivot of Christ's resurrection, and this is what distinguishes Christianity from all religions, including the monotheistic religions of Judaism and Islam, which although they accept the existence of Jesus Christ, they do not accept his resurrection or *deity.*

---

[22] Genesis 6:5 & Romance 3:23
[23] Romance 6:23
[24] Revelation 13:8 & 2 Corinthians 5:21

However, prior to his crucifixion, Jesus himself already declared his *deity* and *power over death* with the miraculous episode recorded in John 11:25–27 (NLT). He boldly said:

'I am the resurrection and the life. Anyone who believes in me will live, even after dying. Everyone who lives in me and believes in me will never ever die. Do you believe this, Martha?'

'Yes, Lord,' she told him. 'I have always believed you are the Messiah, the Son of God, the one who has come into the world from God.'

Did he prove this?

Yes! He supernaturally raised Lazarus, who was dead for four days, back to life[25] to show us that for those who believe in him, physical death or passing away is just *'sleeping'*;[26] it is a transition to be with him forever. Believers shall never really die.

Do you now believe that Jesus is true to who he says he is and that we can trust him?

Like Martha in this scene, it takes perceiving and believing that Christ is the Messiah, the Son of the living God, to make sense of the resurrection. Logical reasoning alone is not enough.

The more I examine the materials of the high priests of the New Atheist Blind Faith Movement, who are Richard Dawkins, Sam

---

25 John 11:39–44 (NLT): "Roll the stone aside," Jesus told them. But Martha, the dead man's sister, protested, "Lord, he has been dead for four days. The smell will be terrible." ... Jesus looked up to heaven and said, "Father, thank you for hearing me. You always hear me, but I said it out loud for the sake of all these people standing here, so that they will believe you sent me." Then Jesus shouted, "Lazarus, come out!" And the dead man came out'.

26 John 11:11 (NLT): 'Our friend Lazarus has fallen asleep, but now I will go and wake him up'.

Harris, Christopher Hitchens, and Daniel Dennett, and their blatant affront and disregard for authentic and accurate historical evidence for the resurrection and anything to do with the supernatural, the more it strengthens my faith in Christ, the risen Lord. Without examining the available literature carefully, these influential atheists, collectively referred to as the '*Four Horsemen*', seem to conclude that the resurrection account is one of the invented stories told to gullible people in an attempt to exploit them.

If, on the historical evidence, sceptics accept that Julius Caesar (a general in the Roman Empire) ever lived, I wonder why they have a problem with the exceedingly more verifiable historical evidence proving that Jesus Christ lived, he was crucified, and rose up from the dead. And for those who only acknowledge his existence, why do you want to stop short of his deity?

Belief in the resurrection and a living Christian God is an intellectually rational proposition held by many highly educated people from all walks of life who have managed to perceive reality beyond just what is accessible through our *five senses* of seeing by the eye or brain, smelling by the nose, tasting by the tongue, touching by the hands, and feeling by the body.

In his excellently-crafted book *Gunning for God*, John Lennox, the emeritus professor of mathematics at the University of Oxford, points out the fallacies in the irrational and unscientific methodology in the ironic belief system of New Atheism. He says it *'provides a classic example of the blind faith it so vocally despises in others.*[27] He also highlights compelling arguments and evidence for Christ's resurrection, and also puts some brilliant new ideas forward about the nature of God and Christianity.

Regarding the authenticity of the resurrection of Jesus, Professor Lennox provides clear historical evidence from reputable sources in a cumulative flow involving accounts for each of

---

[27] John C. Lennox (2011), *Gunning for God: Why the New Atheists Are Missing the Target*, page 15, Oxford, Lion Hudson.

the following:

- The death of Jesus
- The burial of Jesus
- The empty tomb
- The eyewitnesses[28]

On the death of Jesus, he provides:

'The evidence for Jesus' death is so strong . . . is as sure as anything historical can be'. And atheist scholar Gerd Lüdemann wrote: 'Jesus' death as a consequence of crucifixion is indisputable'.[29]

On the burial of Jesus, a man who was an opposing member of the high-profile Jewish *Sanhedrin Council* who decided on the verdict to execute Jesus, took care to give Jesus a decent burial and as an act of courage took a risk by siding with Jesus. *'Joseph of Arimathea, a wealthy man, went to Pilate and requested the body of Jesus to bury it in a tomb that he owned. . . . This account of Pilates's acceding to Joseph's request for the body has all*

[28] From John C. Lennox, page 198.
[29] From John C. Lennox, page 200/201.

the hallmarks of authentic history'.[30] All the four Gospels confirm this and give more information on the guard of Roman soldiers who provided security to prevent any chance of the body from being stolen:

The next day, on the Sabbath, the leading priests and Pharisees went to see Pilate. They told him, 'Sir, we remember what that deceiver once said while he was still alive: "After three days I will rise from the dead." So we request that you seal the tomb until the third day. This will prevent his disciples from coming and stealing his body and then telling everyone he was raised from the dead! If that happens, we'll be worse off than we were at first.

Pilate replied, 'Take guards and secure it the best you can'. So they sealed the tomb and posted guards to protect it (Matt. 27:62–66 NLT).

On the empty tomb:

'The first people to tell the world that the tomb of Jesus was empty were the Jewish authorities and not the Christians at all. They started a story . . . to the effect

---

that the disciples had stolen the body while the guards slept'.[31]

This is found in Matthew 28:11–15 NLT:

As the women were on their way, some of the guards went into the city and told the leading priests what had happened. A meeting with the elders was called, and they decided to give the soldiers a large bribe. They told the soldiers, 'You must say, "Jesus' disciples came during the night while we were sleeping, and they stole his body." If the governor hears about it, we'll stand up for you so you won't get in trouble'. So the guards accepted the bribe and said what they were told to say. Their story spread widely among the Jews, and they still tell it today.

On the eyewitnesses to the resurrection, Lennox wrote:

'It is often said, because the evidence for the resurrection of Jesus Christ comes predominantly from Christian sources, there is a danger of it being partisan, and therefore not carrying the weight of independent

---

[31] From John C. Lennox, page 205.

testimony'.[32]

He discounts this with the argument that although those who were convinced by the evidence for the resurrection became Christians, they were not necessarily Christians when they first heard of the resurrection. One of the best examples is Saul of Tarsus, who later became Paul. Saul was a leading intellectual who tried his best to completely obliterate the resurrection story and annihilate Christianity. Below is his confession:

Dear brothers and sisters, I want you to understand that the gospel message I preach is not based on mere human reasoning. I received my message from no human source, and no one taught me. Instead, I received it by direct revelation from Jesus Christ.

You know what I was like when I followed the Jewish religion—how I violently persecuted God's church. I did my best to destroy it. I was far ahead of my fellow Jews in my zeal for the traditions of my ancestors (Gal. 1:11–14 NLT).

---

[32] From John C. Lennox, page 217.

In light of Paul's background, we can take his witness on the resurrection below as a significant one:

I passed on to you what was most important . . . Christ died for our sins, just as the Scriptures said. He was buried, and he was raised from the dead on the third day . . . He was seen by Peter and then by the Twelve. After that, he was seen by more than 500 of his followers at one time, most of whom are still alive, though some have died. Then he was seen by James and later by all the apostles. Last of all, as though I had been born at the wrong time, I also saw him (1 Cor. 15:3–8 NLT).

Given that high profile court cases today are decided on the account of just one authentic eyewitness, the over 500 eyewitnesses on Christ's resurrection can be taken as a very compelling evidence.

Christ's resurrection, seen by more than 500 people at one time, is also a revelation of our future selves if we believe. *We will have bodies not limited by space, time or matter, and we shall never die* (1 Cor. 15:42–44).

Confronting Life

Like the existence of God, the resurrection cannot be proven by pure logic, but believing is the best we can do to enable us to make sense of the overwhelming complexities in the universe. This may explain why, given the logical improbabilities, some intellectual giants like Immanuel Kant still believed in the existence of God based on practical reason.[33]

Why?

The evidence is inherent *in nature* and also *intuitive on the inside* of each person only if we will listen to that small still voice of conscience.[34]

The human capacity to do science in itself requires an explanation if there is no Creator. Even the demons believe.[35]

For Alister McGrath, a professor of historical theology at the University of Oxford with two degrees in natural sciences who wrote to

[33] From John C. Lennox, page 230.

[34] Romans 1:20—21 (NKJV): 'For since the creation of the world His invisible *attributes* are clearly seen, being understood by the things that are made . . . so that they are without excuse'.

[35] James 2:19 (NKJV): 'Even the demons believe—and tremble!'

challenge Richard Dawkins' book *The God Delusion*, converted from atheism to a believer after carefully investigating what Christianity is. He had this to say to Richard Dawkins:

When I read The God Delusion I was both saddened and troubled. How, I wondered, could such a gifted popularizer of the natural Sciences, who once had such a passionate concern for the objective analysis of evidence, turn into such an aggressive anti-religious propagandist, with an apparent disregard for evidence that was not favourable to his case?[36]

He shares his faith with Dawkins in a mutually respectful conversation on YouTube.[37]

So there is enough evidence to rationally believe in Christ's resurrection but not so much evidence to believe based on reason alone. Some degree of faith is required to experience the power of the resurrection and the resurrected Lord. There are many things we

---

[36] Alister McGrath and Joana C. McGrath (2007), *The Dawkins Delusion: Atheist Fundamentalism and the Denial of the Divine*, London, SFPCK: Page X.
[37] Richard Dawkins debates Alister McGrath on YouTube, available at: https://www.youtube.com/watch?v=bLdsRfkkTf4&t=2296s.

cannot see but we believe they exist. The wind is a good example. Although we cannot see it, we can experience and feel it.

In the natural, there is no logical reason to help wrap our minds around the resurrection. It is okay to have doubts. Even the Disciples doubted[38] when they were initially told about a risen Christ. Thomas, in his scepticism, asked for more evidence.[39] *But the best attitude is to humbly ask God to help us with our struggle to believe,*[40] so the Living Christ will reveal himself to us in some way. He is doing it every day for people who humbly seek to know him.

Are you ready to start this journey today?

---

[38] Luke 24:11 (NKJV): 'And their words seemed to them like idle tales, and they did not believe them'.

[39] John 20:24—29 (NKJV): 'Thomas . . . said to them, "Unless I see in His hands the print of the nails, and put my finger into the print of the nails, and put my hand into His side, I will not believe."'

[40] Mark 9:24 (NKJV): 'Lord . . . help my unbelief!'

Activities based on Question and Answer 3

1. What are your thoughts about Jesus?

2. Why do you or do not believe in Jesus' resurrection?

3. What happens to a person who disregards the obvious evidence for a Creator as stated in Romans 1:20–32?

Question 4: Is Christianity a Kingdom or a religion?

Suggested Answer to Question 4

Among these three keywords: Christianity, Kingdom and religion, *Kingdom*, which is the *Creator's heavenly government influence on earth*, is the oldest and the most important in the context of the Bible. *The Kingdom is God's original idea invented by him at Creation.* It can neither be stopped nor destroyed. It is eternal[41]. However, the first humans (Adam and Eve) lost it due to their rebellion, and its restoration is the reason

---

[41] Daniel 7:18 (NLT): 'But in the end, the holy people of the Most High will be given the kingdom, and they will rule forever and ever.'

why Jesus came to the earth.[42]

Before and after the resurrection, *the Gospel of the Kingdom* was the only or main message Jesus preached and instructed his disciples and followers to preach.[43]

Christianity, based on Christ's sacrificial atonement, his nature, values, principles, and teachings, got started about 50 days after the resurrection.[44] The term *"Christian"* is quite relatively recent. It was coined and first given by pagans in Antioch (modern day Antakya in Turkey) to the followers of Christ[45].

Religion, on the other hand, is a human invention, and what we engage in until we rediscover what we lost (the Kingdom). It is man searching for God. *It is the search we embark*

---

[42] Luke 4:43 (NLT): 'I must preach the Good News of the Kingdom of God in other towns, too, because that is why I was sent'.

[43] Acts 1:3 (NLT, and from Luke 9:2): 'During the forty days after he suffered and died, he appeared to the apostles from time to time, and he proved to them in many ways that he was actually alive. And he talked to them about the Kingdom of God'.

[44] Luke 24:49 (NLT): 'I will send the Holy Spirit, just as my Father promised. But stay here in the city until the Holy Spirit comes and fills you with power from heaven'. This happed in Acts 2.

[45] Acts 11:26 (NLT): '... It was at Antioch that the believers were first called Christians.'

on until we find Christ and the Kingdom that we lost. Check Question 1 to see the void this catastrophic loss of contact and intimate relationship with our Creator created in the human spirit.

In the absence of the Kingdom, every human being on earth is religious whether they embrace institutionalised religion or philosophies like atheism. Do you have scientifically or empirically unproven beliefs erroneously assumed as true like the following?:

"Intellectually capable and emotionally matured modern people do not need God."

All believers in this statement are as religious as any other. In Tim Keller's view, *all moral positions are implicitly religious, and the very call to privatise and get rid of religious beliefs from the public domain is itself religious.*[46]

In his introduction page, Dr Myles Munroe

---

[46] Tim Keller (2008), The Reason for God: Belief in an Age of Scepticism, USA, Penguin Group.

wrote: '*Religion is defined as the adherence to a set of* **beliefs** *that regulate the moral, social, and ritualistic behaviour of the individual*'.[47]

And institutional or organised religion is mankind's attempt to satisfy the inexplicable spiritual craving in the human spirit, and the desire to earn the acceptance, favour and blessing of God **through** doctrinally based rules, traditions and cultural practices. In all religions, adherents have to become their own saviour by achieving some degree of perfection in order to be accepted by the god(s).

Christianity is different. It is not a religion. It has a *saviour* who gives us his righteousness as a gift, a clean slate, and empowers us with the grace to live right when we genuinely put our faith and trust in him, making us become members of his Kingdom – a family in a loving relationship with God. This loving, intimate and personal relationship with the Creator comes through Christ, the King of the

---

[47] Myles Munroe (2006), *Kingdom Principles: Preparing for Kingdom Experience and Expansion*, USA, Destiny Image, (emphasis added).

Kingdom of Heaven.[48]

In the words of Myles Munroe: *'A kingdom is a governing* **influence** *of a* **king** *over his territory, impacting it with his will, his purpose, and his* **intention**, *producing a citizenry of people who express his* **culture** *and reflect his* **nature***'.[49]*

God intends that his influence, purpose, character, and nature of Love[50] (that caused him to create us so he could love us) shall, through mankind, reflect this earth as it is in Heaven. This *was* the original mandate[51] to Adam and Eve and the human race, it was what Jesus came to restore[52], *it is* what we *are* commanded to advance today, and it *will always be* His Kingdom rulership on earth for eternity[53].

---

[48] John 18:33—37 (NKJV): '... Jesus answered, "my kingdom is not of this world"'.

[49] Myles Munroe – 'The Kingdom of God Defined', available on YouTube at: https://www.youtube.com/watch?v=o6EIWJOQ7qY&t=243s , emphasis added.

[50] I John 4:8, 16 (NKJV): 'God is love'.

[51] Genesis 1:26 (NKJV, and Ps. 115:16): 'Then God said, "Let us make man in our image . . . let them have dominion over . . . the earth"'.

[52] Matthew 6:10 (NKJV): 'Your kingdom come. Your will be done on earth as it is in heaven'.

[53] Revelation 5:10 (NKJV): 'And have made us kings and priests to our God; And we shall reign on the earth'.

One case to show Christianity is not a religion but a loving relationship with God in his Kingdom is observable in the life of Saul/Paul. Before he became a Christian, he was a violent, fundamental, religious Pharisee.[54] But after his conversion to Christianity, he learned the character and non-violent nature of King Jesus and recognised that he was no longer in a religion but a Kingdom, and this shows in what he wrote to the Christians at Ephesus:

*'Now, therefore, you are no longer strangers and foreigners, but fellow citizens **[of God's Kingdom]** with the saints and members of the household of God'* (Eph. 2:19 NKJV; emphasis added).

We learn from Paul that religion may divide us but the Kingdom will always unite the entire human race around the nature of the King, which is Love.

Given that human beings are not perfect, there are occasional excesses based on the misunderstanding of the fundamental ethos of

---

[54] Galatians 1:11–15 (NKJV):

Christianity or God's Kingdom, which degenerate into chaos, like the Crusades and human practices and culture in the Bible regretfully used to justify slavery and the subjugation of women. This occasional drift is also true with every system that requires imperfect human beings to operate to keep it functional. For example, organised religion with belief in God has been accused of causing wars in the world. However, *philosophical religion* with no belief in God, like Stalinist Soviet Union, Communist China, and other regimes in their attempt to get rid of organised religion violently oppressed and killed more people in the 20th century than all religious wars combined.[55]

However, Christianity, centred around the ultimate value of Love, is different: it is a *universal Kingdom.* Like Paul, Christians recognise how we have been undeservedly forgiven and accepted to God's Kingdom through King Jesus, so we extend the same

---

[55] Available at: https://www.nybooks.com/daily/2018/02/05/who-killed-more-hitler-stalin-or-mao/.

unconditional love and compassion to all humanity. This was shown by two ex-Muslim girls who blessed and prayed for those who tortured them for their belief in Christ.[56]

Activities based on Question and Answer 4

1. Do you consider Christianity as another religion?

    Why?/Why not?

2. Compare Christianity with or to any one religion.

3. What happens to a person who rejects Jesus?

Question 5: Saved, what next?

Suggested Answer to Question 5

Once we humbly accept Jesus' sacrifice and genuinely trust him for the rest of our lives, all our sins are forgiven, we are justified, we become citizens of God's Kingdom, which originates from Heaven but Jesus brought back to earth, and we start our everlasting life[57] in and with God right now, right here on earth, such that death or passing away is only a transition to the other side of eternity.

Salvation is by God's grace received by faith. We do not deserve it, and we can neither earn

---

[57] John 17:3 (NKJV): 'And this is eternal life, that they may know You, the only true God, and Jesus Christ whom You have sent'.

nor merit it. It is totally free at Christ's expense. Does this suggest there is nothing to do?

There is so much to do but not as a way to earn salvation. We work in response to God's unconditional love, as a demonstration of our faith in Christ, and to earn crowns or rewards in Heaven[58]

The clue to what's next after salvation can be picked up from what Paul wrote to the new Christians in Corinth:

'Now then, we are ambassadors for Christ' (2 Cor. 5:20 NKJV).

The expectation for the rest of the Christian life is to live as ambassadors – authorised representatives of God's government (the Kingdom of Heaven) on this earth.

Just as ambassadors of the United Kingdom are mandated to influence other countries with the intentions of the UK government they are sent to represent, so should all Christians live

---

[58] Revelation 22:12 (NKJV): 'And behold, I am coming quickly, and My reward *is* with Me, to give to every one according to his work.'

with God's mandate to influence the entire earth with his nature of love, his culture, his values and the principles of the Kingdom we are now citizens[59] of.

The following are a few true characteristics of ambassadors:

- They do not live for themselves anymore.
- They do not do their own will or even speak their position on anything but the intentions of their country of citizenship.
- They are trained.
- They are protected and provided for.
- They must be matured, as children cannot be ambassadors.

In this Kingdom, regardless of your age or socioeconomic status, everyone starts as a child. This is the spiritual *born-again experience*,[60] which happens when we genuinely receive Jesus into our heart as our saviour. Then we have to undergo training and grow in the

---

[59] Philippians 3:20 (NKJV): 'For our citizenship is in heaven'.
[60] John 3:3 (NKJV): 'Unless one is born again, he cannot see the kingdom of God'.

knowledge, values, and principles in the Kingdom found in the Bible to know our rights and responsibilities, and how to function as ambassadors.

God expects Christians to be ambassadors of social justice, integrity, love, truth, righteousness, peace and joy[61] to the world. These are some of the nature and values of the non-religious Kingdom we represent, and the King wants his representatives to influence all spheres of the earth and all sectors in every economy (government, education/science & technology, business & finance, entertainment & culture, media, sports, and social & spiritual organisations) with his nature and principles. This way, we are following Christ's instruction to 'occupy'[62] until he comes back.

Will you represent or misrepresent King Jesus?

---

[61] Romans 14:17 (NKJV): 'For the kingdom of God is ... righteousness and peace and joy'.
[62] Luke 19:13b (KJV): 'Occupy till I come'.

Saved, what next?

Activities based on Question and Answer 5

1. Are you saved and have you become a citizen of God's Kingdom?

2. In which specific ways or spheres are you acting non-religiously as an ambassador of God's Kingdom?

3. What happens to a Christian who does not live as an ambassador for Christ?

Saved, what next?

Question 6: What ought to be the priority in life?

Suggested Answer to Question 6

We all do prioritise because time is scarce and our resources are limited while our wants are virtually unlimited, such that it is impossible to do or have everything we wish all at the same time. As a result, we must decide which of our wants should feature at the top of our scale of preference. Some people prioritise their jobs or career above all else. Others put their spouse, children or family first.

It is advisable to check what the Creator of life has to say in the book of life:

*Therefore do not worry, saying, 'What shall we **eat**?'*

What ought to be the priority in life?

*or 'What shall we **drink**?' or 'What shall we **wear**?' For after all these things the Gentiles seek. For your heavenly Father knows that you need all these things.*

But **seek first the kingdom of God and His righteousness***, and all these things shall be added to you (Matt. 6:31–33,* NKJV*, emphasis added).*

It is interesting to notice the contrast between what the Creator wants us to put first versus what human beings actually do put first – food, water, clothing and shelter as discovered by the influential psychologist Abraham Maslow in his *hierarchy of needs model*[63] that recommends these physiological needs as the first set of needs that drive and motivate all human actions. These needs are not to take the top spot in our lives.

Rather, the ultimate value and priority we pursue first should be the *Kingdom*. This concept is made up of two words: *king* and *dominion*, that is, knowing the King, and

---

[63] Maslow's hierarchy of needs – available at:
https://www.bbc.co.uk/news/magazine-23902918.

advancing his influence on earth.

1. Are you diligently seeking to personally discover King Jesus more for yourself?
2. Are you maintaining the righteousness King Jesus gives as a gift[64] at salvation and living righteously?
3. Are you dominating an area or sphere of life with King Jesus' Kingdom principles of love, peace, joy, truth, diligence, excellence, and other Kingdom values?
4. Are you pursuing all of the above as a priority in your life?

If you can sincerely say yes to all the above four questions, you are seeking the Kingdom of God and his righteousness first. You have got the priority right, and you can get ready to expect all other things in life to flow in your way.

Anything we value and love more than the Kingdom, be it money, family, career, fame, or power, becomes the source of our anxiety. This

---

[64] Romans 5:17 (NKJV): 'The gift of righteousness will reign in life through the One, Jesus Christ'.

is self-evidently true because those things can always be lost, but the Kingdom is permanent, omnipresent[65] and everlasting.

How do we advance the Kingdom on earth?

We know that in the Kingdom of Heaven, there is joy.[66] God will wipe away all tears and put an end to suffering.[67]

So any initiative, endeavour or action we use to alleviate or reduce poverty, pain or unnecessary suffering is bringing the Kingdom of God to that place or sphere on earth. Also, acts of Love and Kindness are other ways to bring the Kingdom of God to people.

Jesus practically demonstrated the dominion aspect of the Kingdom by exercising power over nature. He spoke to storms, wind, and trees and got results. *So when we exercise power over*

---

[65] Luke 17:21 (NKJV): 'The kingdom of God is within you'.
[66] Romans 14:17.
[67] Revelation 21:4 (NKJV): 'God will wipe away every tear from their eyes; there shall be no more death, nor sorrow, nor crying'.

nature through scientific exploration and discoveries to alleviate suffering, we are manifesting the Kingdom. This is what led the early Kingdom-minded Christians to invent the hospital and university.[68]

The Kingdom is the King's domain. So without the King, the dominion we exercise does not bring fulfilment. For example, Kanye West tried to dominate the music industry without King Jesus. The outcome was inalienable internal and external suffering until he sought after and found the King and began the advancement of his Kingdom to reach the sphere of entertainment so he eventually started to experience true joy. Below are some quotes from him:

- *'Those who are not in service to God are in service to everything else'.*
- *'When you remove the love and fear of God, you create the love and fear of everything'*
- *'To be radically in service to Christ is the only culture I want to know about'*

---

[68] Rebecca McLaughlin (2019), *Confronting Christianity: 12 Hard Questions for the World's Largest Religions*, Wheaton, Crossway Books.

What ought to be the priority in life?

- *'To live inside of sin, it's going to cost you more than you can pay'.*
- *'I understand that people feel that I've made some cultural sins. But the only real sins are the sins against God, and you don't want to continue to sin against God'.*
- *'I'm still here! "Jesus is King" [music album] was No. 1'.*[69]

So the priority of life is to seek to embody the King's character, nature and personality, to maintain our right standing with him, and to act as ambassadors of his Kingdom to influence a sphere(s) of the earth.

When we do this, the able and faithful King fully takes care of us.

---

[69] Kanye West's statements, available online at:
https://www1.cbn.com/cbnnews/entertainment/2020/april/lsquo-i-rsquo-m-definitely-born-again-rsquo-kanye-west-opens-up-about-his-faith-importance-of-christians-speaking-up, emphasis added.

Activities based on Question and Answer 6

1. Have you made King Jesus a priority, and do you constantly and personally seek to discover him more every day?

2. Which area(s) are you bringing in Jesus' Kingdom (influence) to people so his Kingdom will positively impact that part of the earth?

3. What happens to a person who rejects the Kingdom?

What ought to be the priority in life?

Question 7: What is the best view of success?

Suggested Answer to Question 7

There is an innate desire in the human soul to be successful. From Napoleon Hill's classic book *Think and Grow Rich*, through *The Success Principles* by Jack Canfield, *Rich Dad Poor Dad* by Robert T. Kiyosaki, *The One Minute Millionaire* by Mark Hansen and Robert Allen, and *The Automatic Millionaire Homeowner* by David Bach, just to mention a few in no particular order, all appear to perceive success as a *personal accomplishment* of some sort in an area in life, thereby making *success* an expansive word that could mean financial success, educational success, family success, career success, personal health success, or an achievement of a set goal in life. For example, if a person achieves a goal to become the first in their family history to attain a PhD, this is educational success to them.

Although these great books are effective in producing outstanding results if the principles these high-achieving authors espouse are followed, the material or personal attainment does not seem to be a true view of success as happiness and fulfilment that accompany real success appears to elude many with the most career and financial success. Statistics from the USA reveal that '*most suicides are . . . by the people in the circle of Hollywood millionaires*'.[70]

The best view of success is found in a profound statement the ultimate model of life made:

'*I have **glorified You** on the earth. I have **finished the work** which You have given Me to do*' (John 17:4

---

[70] Sunday Adelaja (2016), *How to Keep Your Focus*, Milton Keynes, Golden Pen Ltd., Page 14.

NKJV, emphasis added).

This statement, made by Christ just before the crucifixion, conveys so much truth:

- Every individual life is sent by God to this world to accomplish a specific purpose (work), that needs to be discovered.
- Success is when this assignment is discovered and executed well.
- The execution of the assigned purpose brings glory to God by promoting his grand will and intention for the human race on this earth

Such that when we stand before the Creator at the end of our life to give account,[71] we can say yes to the following two statements:

- *'I glorified you while I was on earth.'*
- *'I discovered, pursued and finished the work you sent me to earth to do.'*

---

[71] Romans 14:12 (NKJV): 'So then each of us shall give account of himself to God'.

So true success is not how long we live, how much money we acquire, or how many trophies or certificates of honour we obtain. It is not even about career or family. As essentially important as all of these are, they remain here on earth as shadows and golden statues unless they facilitate the fulfilment of purpose.

True success is to approach life like Jesus – to focus on purpose and excel in executing it with the aim of glorifying God and blessing people in a sphere of our influence, like education, business, sport, music, and the rest. This is exactly what happened to Mark Koch, who did not find true success in the height of his glamorous career as a Hollywood movie producer, but rather in his purpose to advance God's Kingdom through movies and his book *The First Hour.*[72]

The **universal purpose for all mankind** is to

---

[72] Mark Koch's story, available at: https://thefirsthour.com/.

reveal God's Love and Creativity to people to make this world a better place so it reflects his Heavenly Kingdom. Every individual has their specific role to play in this grand mission for the human race on earth. I, therefore, define purpose or my role or work as follows:

'My purpose is the **primary reason** *I was born. It is* **my unique assignment** *designed* **by God for his Kingdom and Glory**, *to be* **discovered** *and executed with excellence to* **serve humanity**, *and by so doing, derive my* **fulfilment**'.

And success, that will outlast this temporary world and count in eternity, is how well I carry out this pre-ordained assignment.[73]

The highest form of glory or worship we can ever give God is when we honour his purpose for our life and fulfil it; that is the work He sent us here to do. Therefore, the most important pursuit in life should be the discovery of purpose. It is in the pursuit of purpose that we find true meaning, fulfilment and joy in this life, despite the

---

[73] Jeremiah 1:5 (NKJV): 'Before I formed you in the womb I . . . ordained you . . . to the nations'.

suffering and uncertainty.

The problem in the world today, the meaning crises around the Western world in particular in the midst of plenty and high economic and material well-being, can be traced to the fact that most people are stuck to their jobs and have built their life around them at the expense of their purpose, their true work. Our job or career, although it can be done purposefully, in most cases may not be our assignment or purpose. The following are a few contrasts about a job and purpose:

- Our job is what the school system trains us to do, while our purpose is what we were born and naturally gifted to do.
- Our job helps us to pay our bills, while our purpose brings a blessing and true success.
- Our job may frustrate us, but our purpose gives us fulfilment.

How do I discover my purpose?

The best way is to just ask the Creator, '*What did you send me here for?*' and then listen from within because the assignment is buried on the inside of us. When we totally give our life to him as a living sacrifice and renew our mind with the values and principles of his Kingdom, he shows us his desires and will for our lives.

Another way is to carefully study our ***SHAPE***, which is pastor Rick Warren's acronym for:

Spiritual gifts:

- Discovered by studying what God has supernaturally gifted you to do

Heart:

- What you have a burning desire, love and passion for

Abilities:

- What natural talents you are born with, and the skills you have acquired

Personality:

- What your personality is and where you can best serve with it

Experiences:

- What painful, spiritual, educational or life experiences you have been exposed to and how you can best use them to serve

Our **SHAPE** is given by God to bring him glory by serving people. Therefore, a person will be truly successful and most effective when they use their **S**piritual gifts and **A**bilities in the area of their **H**eart's desire, and in a way that best expresses their **P**ersonality and **E**xperiences to glorify God by serving people with his Kingdom values of love, peace, joy, righteousness and truth.

According to pastor Rick Warren, *the better the fit of our* **SHAPE** *to the service we are engaged in (purpose), the more successful we will be.*[74] This way

---

[74] Rick Warren (2002), *The Purpose Driven Life: What on Earth Am I Here For?*, Michigan, Zondervan, Page 248.

we can unashamedly say to the Creator at the end of our life here, 'I glorified you and finished the work you gave me to do'. This is the best view of true success!

Activities based on Question and Answer 7

1. What is your view of success?

2. Have you discovered your purpose?

3. What happens to a person who never discovers their primary purpose – the reason why God sent them here?

Answers to Activities Questions

Activities based on Question and Answer 1

1. *Like this Samaritan woman, do you want to accept Jesus' free offer?*

If yes, then be sincere with him and talk to him.

Thank him for the opportunity to know him.

Tell him that you acknowledge that you are a sinner and need him, and ask him to forgive you of all your sins and help you accept his righteousness by faith.

Invite him to come into your heart and to help you live the rest of your life following him.

If you sincerely mean it from your heart (Rom. 10:9–10), you are brand-new on the inside in your spirit (2 Cor. 5:17) and you need time to start manifesting this new life out in the flesh by first renewing your mind with the truths in the Word of God (Rom. 12:2).

I recommend reading the Book of John in the Bible as a start with Jesus, followed by Genesis, Romans, and Proverbs.

Try to find a small group of believers you can share with or a good Bible-believing church.

2. *Why do you need Jesus?*

We find true and eternal life in him. Through his sacrificial atonement for our sins, he helps us connect to our source (God) and relate to God as a Father.

We will remain thirsty, lacking true satisfaction without him.

3. *What happens to life without Jesus?*

No life, only survival, no purpose, no fulfilment, no authentic peace and joy, no everlasting life.

Activities based on Question and Answer 2

1. *What is the danger for a person who does not discover the phenomenological truth in Christ in the Bible for themselves?*

The Truth in Christ is the light of life, so anyone without Christ is figuratively groping in darkness.[75] Although such people have sight, they still live in darkness. They cannot see who they really are and their purpose.

The light in Christ is more powerful than any form of darkness – both literally and figuratively.

2. *How were our ancestors able to survive without much knowledge of scientific or objective truth?*

It seems like scientific truth is essentially important; it has brought about significant improvement in material well-being, but it is not indispensable for survival and does not

---

[75] From John 1:4 (NKJV): 'In him was life, and the life was the light of men'.

help us with the question of how to live and issues such as purpose, meaning and morality.

It looks to me as if scientific truth helps explain the set stage and objects on the stage of life, but does not inform us of the real purpose of the stage. The stage is the means to an end, which is the drama of life, and the hero of this drama is Christ, who we can all emulate.

3. *List three lessons you have learned, and show how you are going to apply them to your life.*

Answering this personal question helps to experience the Truth in Christ.

Activities based on Question and Answer 3

1. What are your thoughts about Jesus?

Answering this personal question helps to experience the Truth in Christ.

2. Why do you or do you not believe in Jesus' resurrection?

Answering this personal question helps to experience the Truth in Christ.

3. What happens to a person who disregards the obvious evidence for a Creator as stated in Romans 1:20–32?

God will give such people up to follow their subjective feelings and inordinate desires.

The natural consequence of such a wilful, free choice is inalienable suffering and death.

Can you see evidence around you?

Activities based on Question and Answer 4

1. Do you consider Christianity another religion?

Why?/Why not?

You will need to provide some explanation either way.

2. Compare Christianity with or to any one religion.

This will allow you to clearly notice how distinct Christianity is.

- Compare the founders.
- Do they need their sins to be forgiven?
- Did they claim they are God or the Truth or just speak about the truth?
- Did they resurrect from the dead?
- Were their birth, life, resurrection, etc. prophesied?

3. What happens to a person who rejects Jesus?

In John 14:16, Jesus said he is **the** way to God the Father. This is so because it takes Jesus' sacrifice to fully pay for the sin that separates human beings from God. Although Jesus is the only way, there may be many ways to Jesus.

By rejecting Jesus, we are, by default, wilfully choosing death over life (John 10:10), and the devil, who is already judged.

Activities based on Question and Answer 5

1. *Are you saved and have you become a citizen of God's Kingdom?*

If you are yet to accept Jesus as your Lord and saviour, I will suggest the following scriptures for you to consider:

- John 1:12
- Romans 10:9–10

The words you say to salvation have to come sincerely from your heart. In other words, you have to be convinced, convicted and converted. Convinced about Christ, convicted by the Holy Spirit to see your need for a saviour, and then be converted to a brand-new person who is totally forgiven, redeemed, justified and empowered in your spirit. People will know the evidence of this born-again experience by your fruits which may take time to manifest.

2. In which specific ways or spheres are you acting non-religiously as an ambassador of God's Kingdom?

Are all your actions a reflection of God's nature of Love to others? Is this evident in our careers and professions so non-believers will want to find out our motivation?

3. What happens to a Christian who does not live as an ambassador for Christ?

Such a Christian is selfish and remains a child. Such people miss out on their rights and privileges and are unable to enjoy the full benefits of the Kingdom right here on earth (Gal. 4:1–3).

They may go to heaven, but will have no rewards (1 Cor. 3:15).

It is questionable to claim Jesus as your Lord and not obey his instructions to act as light in this dark world (Matt. 5:14, 16).

Activities based on Question and Answer 6

1. *Have you made King Jesus a priority, and are you constantly and personally seeking to discover him more every day?*

Answering this personal question helps to experience the Truth in Christ.

2. *Which area(s) are you bringing in Jesus' Kingdom (influence) to people so his Kingdom will positively impact that part of the earth?*

God wants his influence in every aspect of life: families, education, politics, media, business, entertainment, sports, etc.

3. *What happens to a person who rejects the Kingdom?*

No true joy or fulfilment right here on earth.

No eternal life.

Such people may have only religion, but no true, living, intimate and personal relationship with the King of the Kingdom.

Activities based on Question and Answer 7

1. What is your view of success?

The best is to see life and success through Christ, our ultimate ideal.

He reveals success as finding your purpose and using it to glorify God by serving people.

2. Have you discovered your purpose?

Purpose is the most important pursuit in life.

True joy, fulfilment and productive results are signs to confirm that your vocational pursuit is your primary purpose.

If you are not sure, carefully study your SHAPE.

3. What happens to a person who never discovers their primary purpose – the reason why God sent them here?

No true fulfilment.

It is selfish and a wasted life, depriving many people in this world.

It is failure in the eyes of God regardless of the achievements we get in life. It's just like writing a good answer to the wrong question in an exam.

They may not receive any rewards in eternity (1 Cor. 3:14–15).

About the Author

 John Adjei is a British-Ghanaian author who has been an educator in higher education in the United Kingdom for more than 10 years. He currently teaches economics on pathway programmes at Newcastle University London. His teaching excellence recently earned him the title of Pathway Teacher of the Year 2018.

In addition to his professional ACCA qualification, he holds a master's degree in economics of globalisation and European integration, awarded by a consortium of nine global universities.

He has discovered his purpose in life and has a genuine passion to share this with the world, to make life a little better for everyone.

As parents, John and Linda have raised three

thriving children. They are still constantly learning and turning their knowledge and experience into strategies and tools to help parents on their own journey, and to be advocates for both children and their guardians. John shares the success principles he has discovered, in his books, workshops, and seminars.

For speaking engagements, please contact him at John.Adjei@livingyourbest.co.uk or learn more about him at www.livingyourbest.co.uk.

Below is the other book by the author on Amazon, available at: **https://Author.to/AmazonParentingYourBest**

Parenting Your Best

THE ESSENTIAL AND PRACTICAL GUIDE TO RAISING CHILDREN TO BECOME THEIR BEST

JOHN ADJEI

Printed in Great Britain
by Amazon